Imaginary Press

Email:
capricegeddes@gmail.com

Ordering Information:
Quantity sales. Special discounts are available on quantity purchases by corporations, associations, and others. For details, contact the publisher at the address above.
Orders by U.S. trade bookstores and wholesalers. Please contact the publisher's details above.

Printed in the United States of America

Little Grey Box
Written and Illustrated
by
Caprice Geddes

Acknowledgements

To the people who make me smile and laugh each day, I dedicate this book to you, for you have left me with hope for this world that is filled with a new challenge each way I look.

But thanks to you, each corner I turn I now see you all waiting for me with open arms instead of the loneliness many know.

This book is not just for the people who bring me joy, but for the people who don't have a voice for themselves yet, too scared to speak their mind for fear of being alone. These topics I have chosen to base this on are my own experiences but mainly others who have asked me to raise awareness for the subjects that people are still afraid to discuss on their own.

Whoever reads this book, I hope that you no longer feel alone in an empty corner, there is a community filled with troubled souls who have not yet found their voice enclosed in their little grey box.

I hope I have given you one among the pages.

Little Grey Box

We never quite know someone.

For the people who cause the most harm

Are always closest to you.

- Caprice Geddes

They intend on breaking you down,

making you feel as though

You're only worth as much

As the soil under their feet.

But their only source of a weapon

being their words

And whispers inside your head

Twisting and turning you

In every which way.

Yet we forget that people

Can be as fragile as glass

And break with the touch

Of a finger.

Not willing to acknowledge

That simple phrase,

"We are all not the same,"

Has led us to deal with the biggest

Tragedies of all.

-    Caprice Geddes

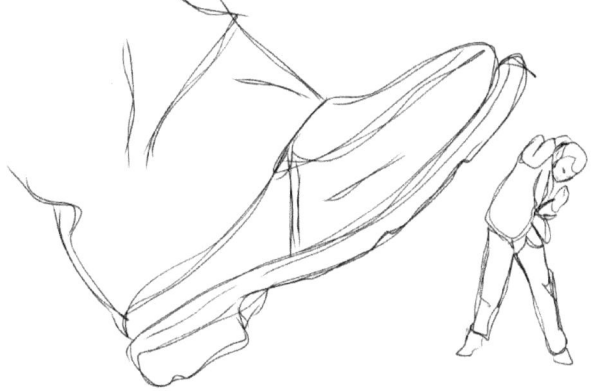

-

There is a woman who can go through hell

And still come out shinning brighter

Then the sun.

Survived the scars that aren't visible

With an individual story of her own.

Has taken on the mess

To save you from the challenges

Life may throw your way.

Yet she refuses to allow this to

Destroy her softness.

We call her our mother.

-   Caprice Geddes

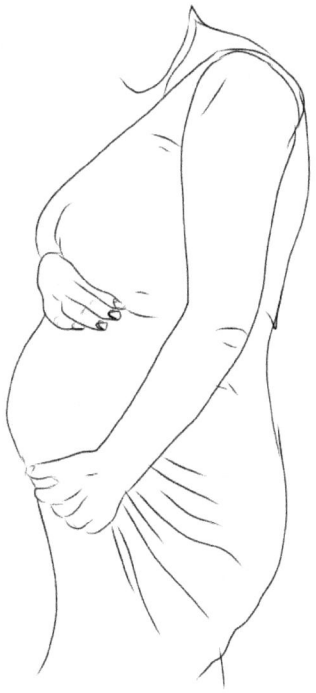

Protect children not guns,

As they have the power to kill

And children have the power

Of love and innocence

So rarely occupying a space in our world.

- Caprice Geddes

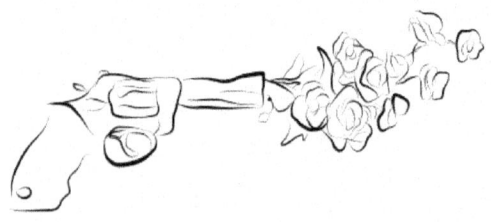

To the man I called Father.

You have taught me not to trust,

To fear the touch of another man,

That to love we must abide

By the rules and step on eggshells

To avoid controversy.

You have taught me that my smile

Will be dulled by the shadowing

Of a men's presence.

That the sparkle in my eyes

Will disappear as I loose

Faith in the opposite gender.

You have ruined the innocence and

Destroyed the love

I once carried.

All because the value of yourself

Was above all others.

-    Caprice Geddes

They've decided that our bodies

Are owned by men,

Only for them to play and tend.

Putting us in fear of the words,

"Not today" to venture from our mouth,

As we know all too well their intentions

Will turn south.

-    Caprice Geddes

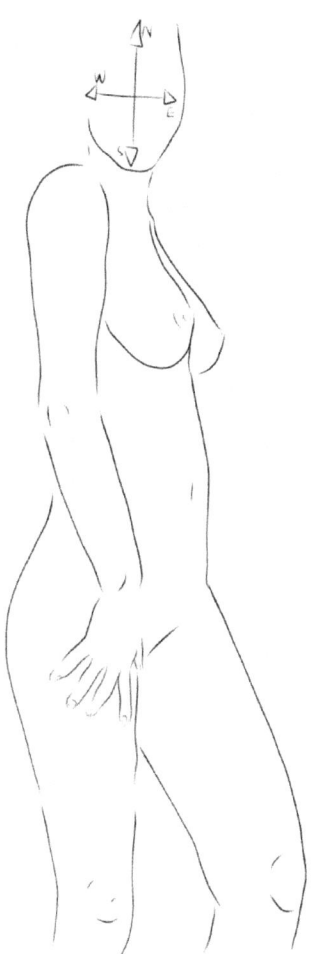

I was running.

Running away from the past,

Running towards the future,

Clasping freedom within my hands

As it was the last.

But as does water

It slipped right through the cracks,

Forever Soaked into the soil

Of the footprints I left in my tracks.

- Caprice Geddes

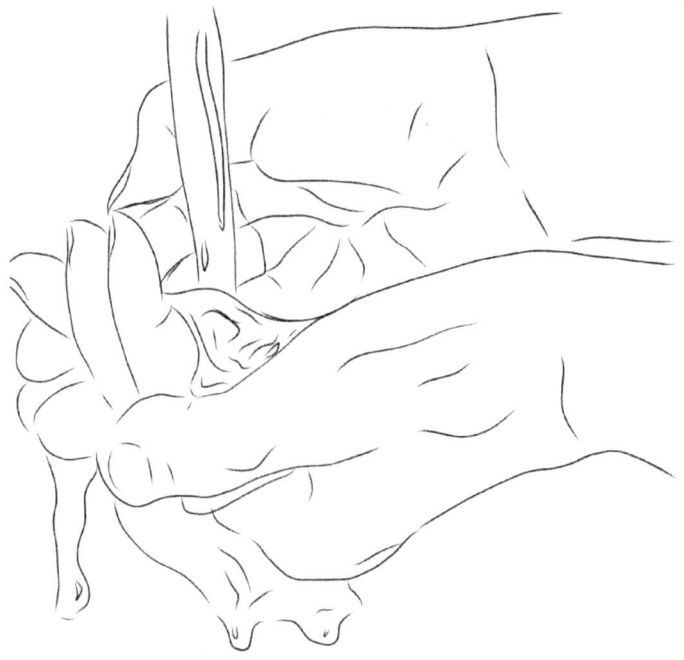

People's opinions do not define you.

You have the ability to construct who you are

And the way you ought to be.

Don't dare allow anyone

Control what you dream.

For they do not walk in your skin

Or in your shoes.

Only becoming happy

As long as you lose.

They feed from the love of the

Pain you provide.

But please for the love of yourself

Place them off to the side.

- Caprice Geddes

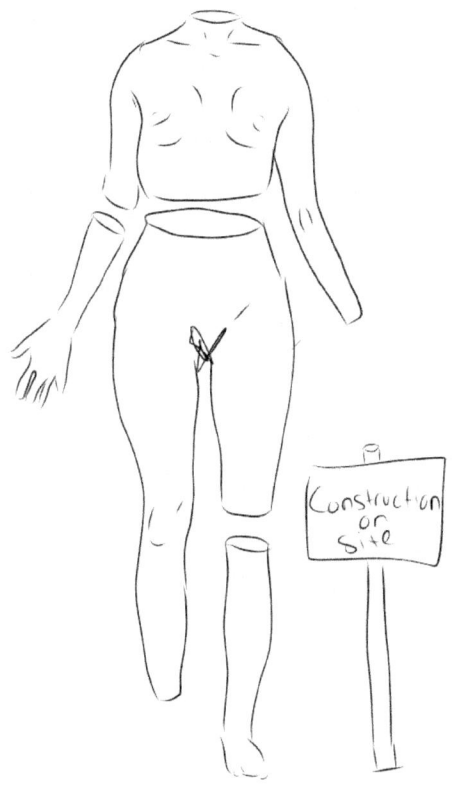

I'm sorry.

I'm sorry to all the girls

who are only noticed for their looks.

I'm sorry that we have not first acknowledged

Your integrity and kindness above all else.

I'm sorry to all the boys

Who are classified under the term

'Fuck Boy' for the reasoning of being simply attractive

In the eyes of one other,

Before knowing your loyalty and dedication.

I'm sorry we have not yet realized as a generation

That personality can speak the truth we

All refuse to hear.

-    Caprice Geddes

'Thick', 'Thicc', 'Thic'.

However you may spell or pronounce it,

It means the same thing.

Do not just now acknowledge the curvy

As we should not take a step back

With the shaming of body size.

The models who were once called beautiful

Are now called appalling.

The size we once thought of as appalling

Is now the only beauty.

We are all to be known as unique,

For who wants to hold the same

Beauty as everyone else.

What a boring world that would be indeed.

- Caprice Geddes

We will only know our reality is beautiful

If it appears within our dreams.

For our brains speak the truly peaceful

At night as we lay asleep it seems.

And if the peaceful picture

Is of a men or women

Who brings you such joy,

They will appear in the universe you created

Not able to destroy.

And if the peaceful is a picture

Of such astounding land,

You are now dreaming

Of the world we wish was as grand.

-     Caprice Geddes

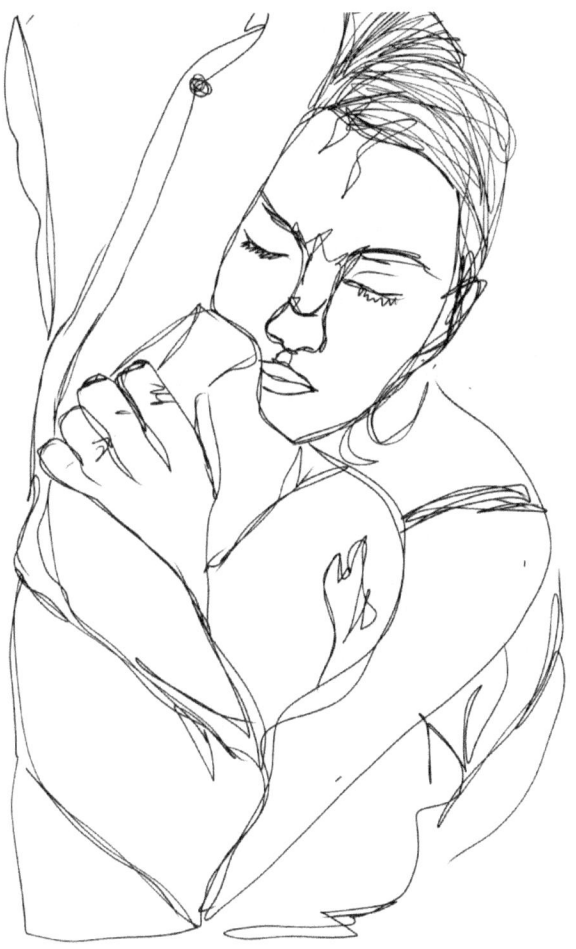

Silence was her medication,

The one that would never wear out,

As her words only turned into disintegration

There was no reason to shout.

Not to shout for help

Not to shout for kindness

As she only felt

Such bitter silence.

Quiet would be her never ending peace

But we all know too well her misery would increase.

-    Caprice Geddes

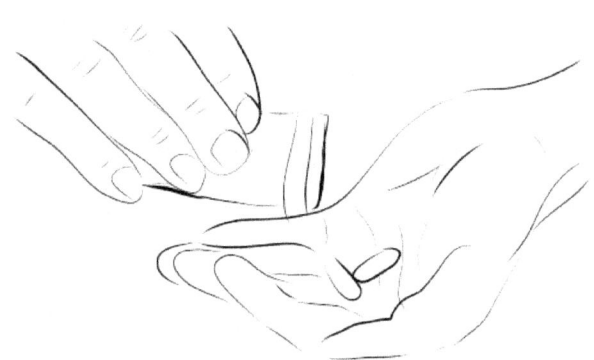

Remember that time when you were younger

And the games played were:

"Ditch your friend in the bathroom"

Or, "let's see how long It takes for them to find us".

A petty little game that seemed to bring

Others so much joy.

Years later and nothing has changed.

We like to think of ourselves as grown and mature,

Changing from the younger stage that used to be vacant.

We've evolved in many ways yes,

But instead of running away from the kids

whose presence was unwanted,

We run away from the very problems

That leave our world flawed.

-    Caprice Geddes

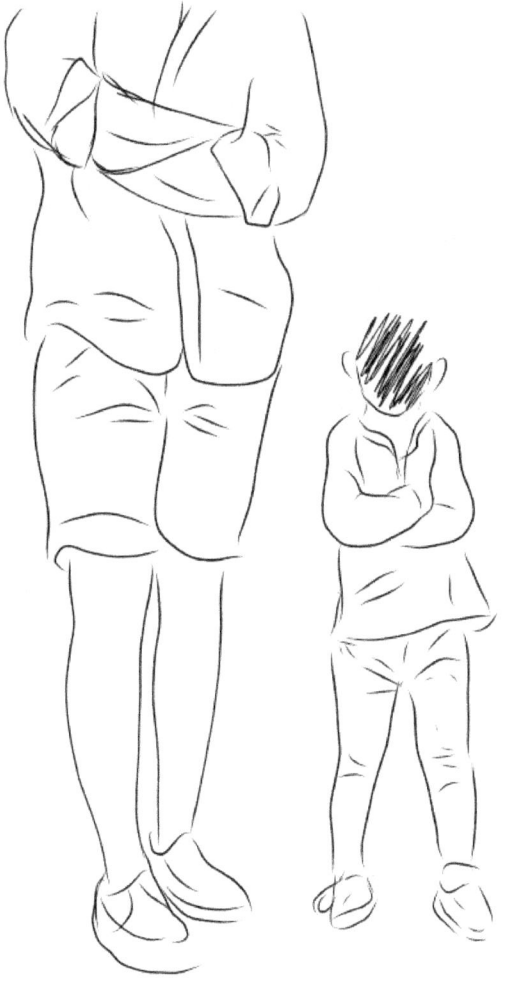

I used to believe I was nothing.

That I'd continue to be represented

By such a short word.

But I am more then I was

And I will continue to grow

Until that word is no longer

What I thought I was, but rather a foe.

-     Caprice Geddes

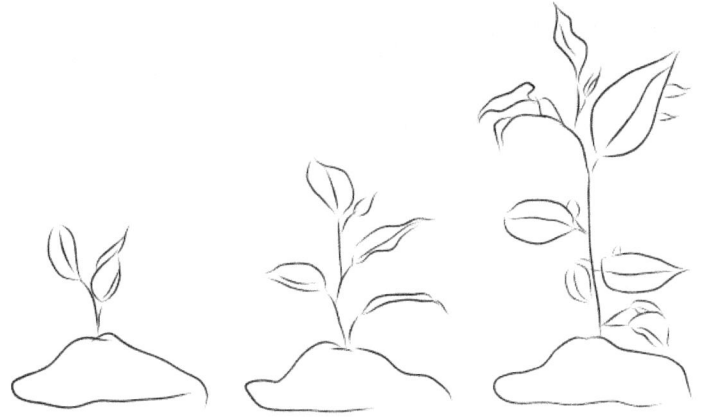

'Beauty is pain', I was told the first time I got my ears pierced.

'Beauty is pain', I was told the first time bleaching my hair.

'Beauty is pain', I was told by the nail salon the first time getting acrylics.

'Beauty is pain', I was told the first time getting my eyebrows waxed.

But what they don't tell you is that the pain isn't physical.

It is a mental illness we have been equipped with since the age we could understand.

We believe that to be societies standard of beauty we require money, makeup and pain.

What happened to the beauty on the inside being attractive.

Not the handmade objects we glue to our irritated skin from years of mistreatment.

We wish to believe that our natural beauty can be more then something fake,

Yet we dull our skin with too light or dark foundation

And cover up what makes us human,

Adding powdered colour to showcase that we still have life to our cheeks

And that our hair shall not grow boring.

-   Caprice Geddes

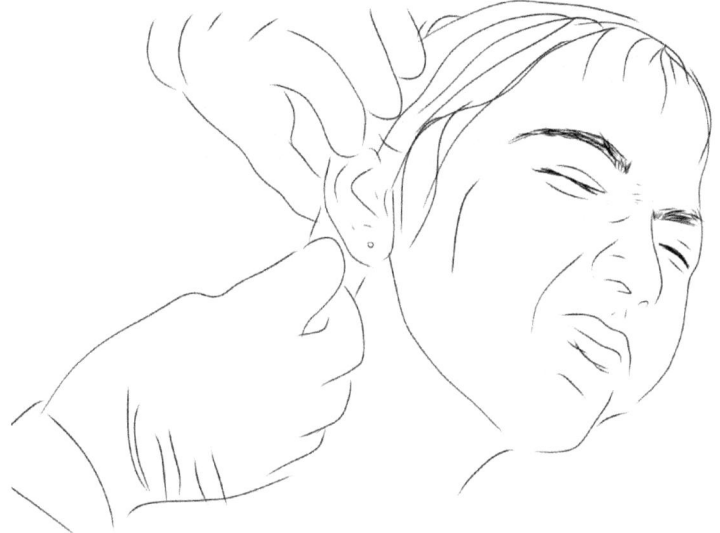

So much time and money spent

For such little feeling of

Happiness.

- Caprice Geddes

She who has not grown cold

As she was alone growing old.

- Caprice Geddes

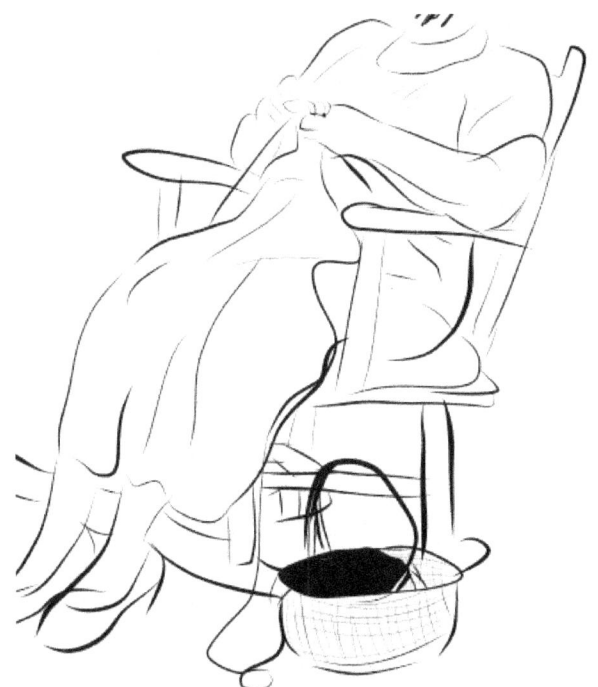

Be fearless.

As you come in contact with the judge

You'll be seen by the millions of people

Scattered around their TV,

Waiting for their friend or family member

To be viewed as a liar or

Someone brave enough to stand

Up to what they have feared for years.

But you must remember little deer,

Bears don't like to back down.

He will have the 13 sat to the side fooled

With glasses, a suit and a rehearsed speech

But nothing will compare to the sheer terror

In your voice as you recall the seconds that changed everything.

-     Caprice Geddes

You have seen better days.

I'm sorry that we, as a whole,

Could not make every

Sunrise to sundown

As glorious as the rest.

But for the angels

That surround you at night

As you fall soundly asleep,

They are trying everything

but their worst at

Keeping you at peace.

- Caprice Geddes

I'd rather happiness over money,

Kindness over luxury

And picked flowers over diamonds.

I'd rather you give me your love

As that is worth more than the worlds

Fortune could provide me with.

-    Caprice Geddes

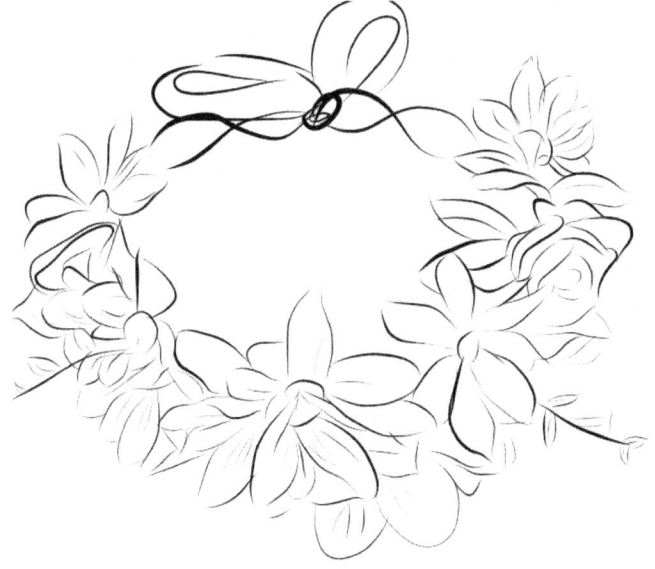

These are frightful times

As we do not know what future awaits us.

But we can be our own fortune tellers

Not needing to pay money for a lady with a crystal ball

To show us the image that decides what we will become,

For we know by our own mistakes

that they have helped shape who we are.

We shall own the right to depict our pathway

For our mistakes lead us down a glorious road

Showing us what to avoid and what we can achieve,

As it is not realistic to just follow a yellow brick road.

- Caprice Geddes

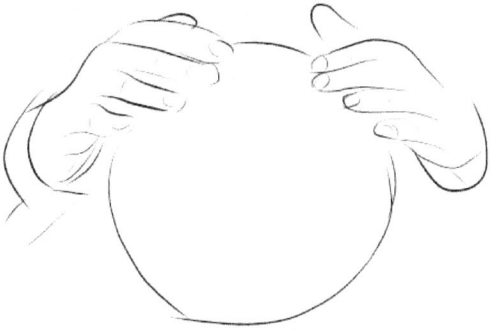

Spread the word of kindness,

As not everyone has felt the touch of a hand that didn't mark

Or those of a voice that didn't send shivers down their spine.

- Caprice Geddes

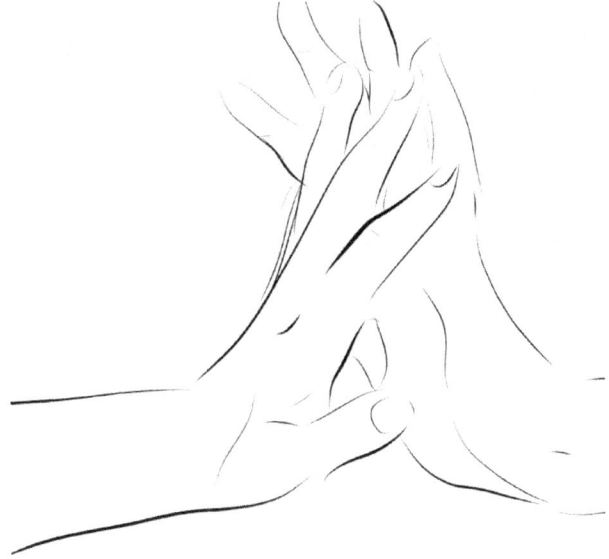

There is a constant war in my mind

Of the dark in the light.

The happiness a split decision could bring

And the cloud of grey that would over shadow it.

-    Caprice Geddes

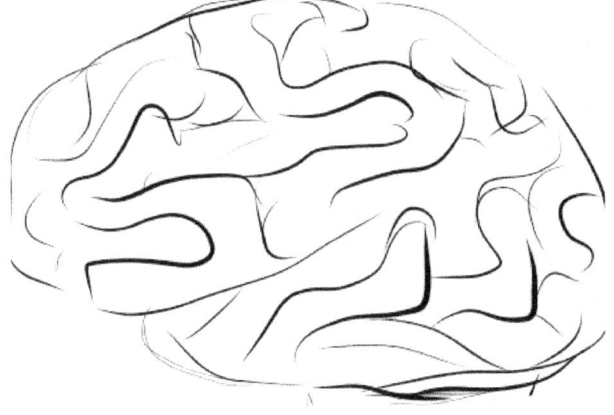

The spreading of wings and the ability to glide over

Land of such beauty seems incredible.

The freedom a bird grasps is so powerful yet

Sad in a sense.

They are so much more powerful within a group

And the way they work together is astounding.

Unfortunately, we do not have wings.

We cannot depend on one another to be there

When we fall.

-    Caprice Geddes

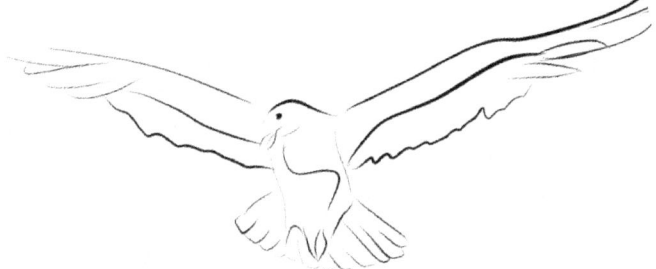

I am not bought nor invested in.

I am not your property for you to bargain with.

-    Caprice Geddes

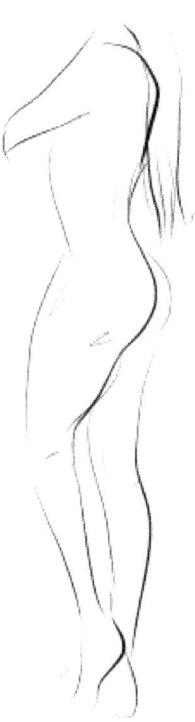

I have now become known as another statistic

Recorded down in the books to add to the

Talks to younger children to understand the signs.

For my life's past has now become one of the many

To scare people into leaving their bad habits.

For you don't want to end up like her.

-    Caprice Geddes

Happiness is described as perfection of human nature,

Yet I have heard 'Happiness is a virtue' more than I can remember

As we cannot seem to achieve such a goal until

Bodies have been put to rest and free of the

Cruelty our word may release.

-     Caprice Geddes

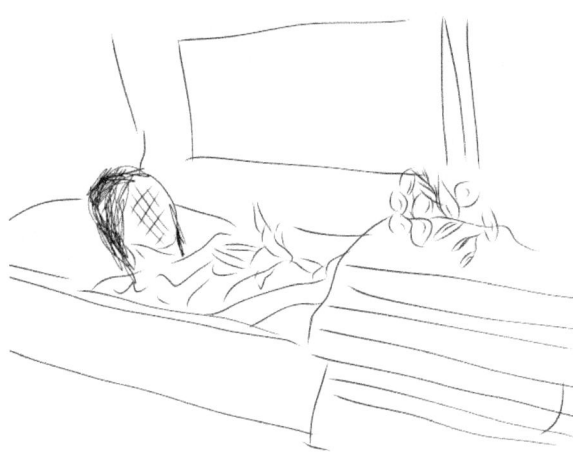

I worked till my eyes hurt

To run home with my report card

For my mum to pin on the blue fridge.

Seeing her so proud was a feeling

Unlike any other.

Putting every bit of energy I had into my work

Was something I did

For a future job that will provide me with the money

I never knew of as a child.

To be something that would make my mother more

Proud then a piece of paper on the fridge.

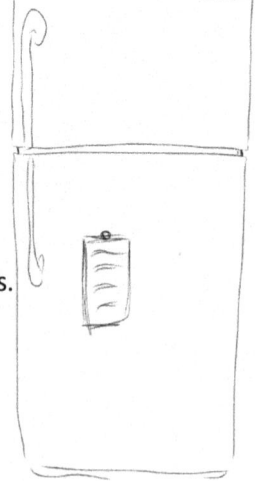

Yet we who work for what we want

Are only classified as a 'try hard'.

That to be popular we must be lazy

And watch our future slip through our hands.

-     Caprice Geddes

You are a ship sailing

Destined for discovery

Of a place not worth bailing

Filled with kindness and recovery.

- Caprice Geddes

My art spoke the words

My mouth could never say.

- Caprice Geddes

Please don't leave me in the dirt,

As you brought me hope in the darkest

Moments and gave me the love

I needed to heal my broken heart

From the loss of shelter

A father provides for his daughter.

- Caprice Geddes

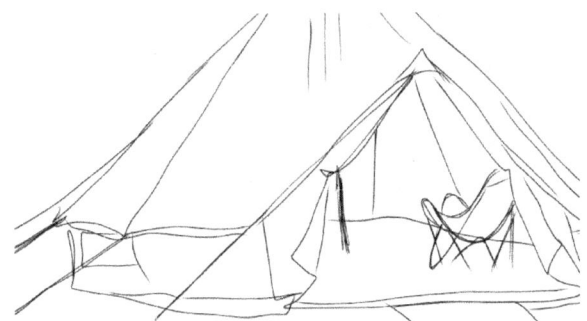

Let them in.

For if they really love you,

They'll appreciate the beauty in the scars not visible,

Fixing the damage others left behind

Far beneath the skin.

-    Caprice Geddes

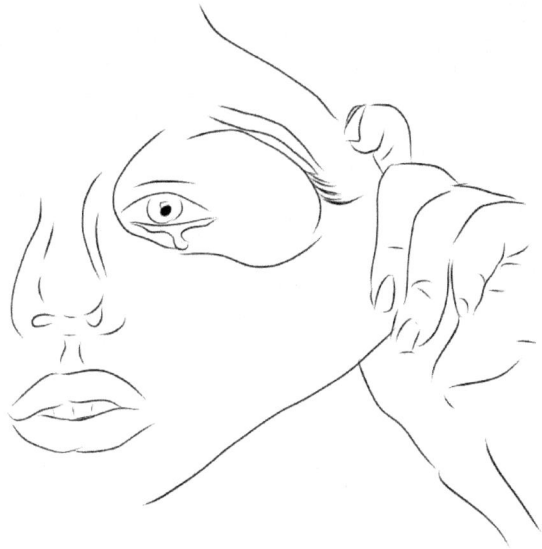

As children we were happy with a small house made of sheets

And your parent's wooden chairs placed corner to corner

To lift the middle for blankets, pillows and

Your favourite colouring books.

That was enough to bring you joy for days on end.

Now we wish for sheets made of bamboo hugging

King sized beds placed in the middle of glassed filled walls

And pretty things to be seen in every corner of the room.

Yet it's the little things in life that bring me the happiest memories.

- Caprice Geddes

Little Grey Box

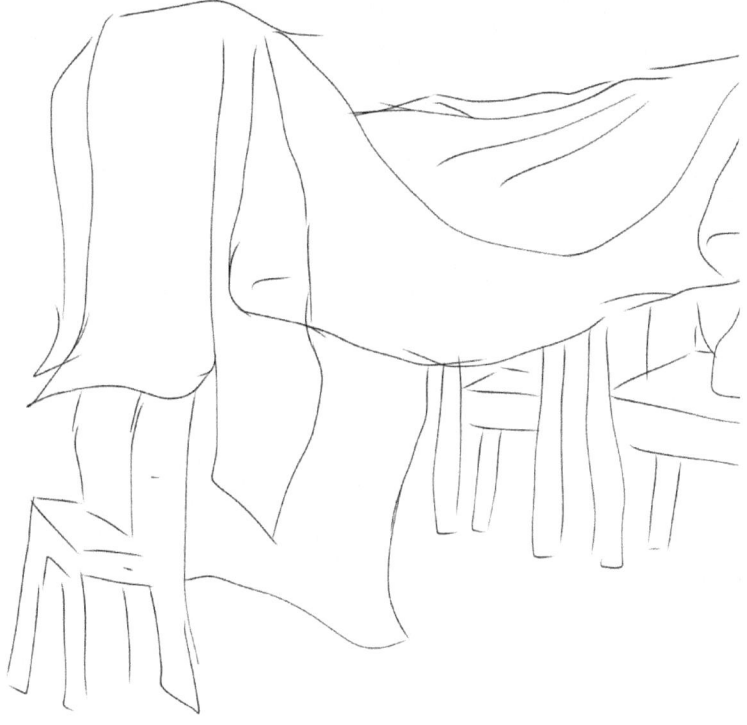

55

He who created a rippling effect

As if he was the unnoticed droplets

Dripping from a tap.

For no one payed attention

On how far we had pushed the handle.

    -    Caprice Geddes

She was soft to the touch

But you shall never know,

For a shadow had her in his clutch

And will never let her go.

-     Caprice Geddes

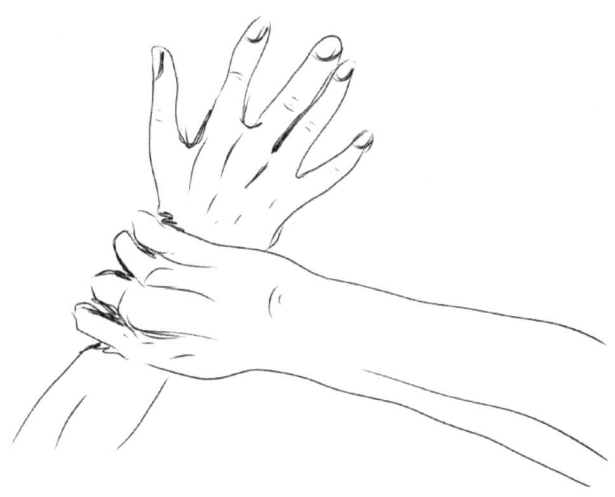

We were taught to live and learn

But I will never be taught to forget

As I am forced to forgive.

- Caprice Geddes

Play the victim,

For that is what you do best my dear,

But do not expect wanted wisdom

As you shed another tear.

I have given you nothing but my all

As no one provided you with much loving.

But I am not your basketball.

I will not continue to bounce back.

-    Caprice Geddes

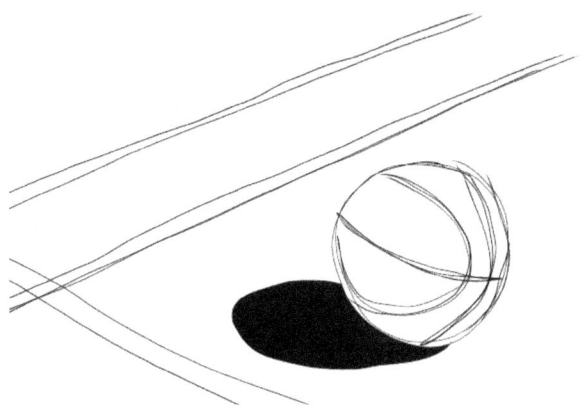

I hated the shade of blue and all It represented.

A melancholy colour I used to demonstrate sadness

And tragedy experienced as my bushes touched paper.

I forgot that it's the shade of one's eyes that brings me

The happiest of memories and the colour of water

That hides such wonder of the world beneath.

It is no longer a colour I wish to bring peoples hatred towards.

It's a shade that has shown me such beauty.

-     Caprice Geddes

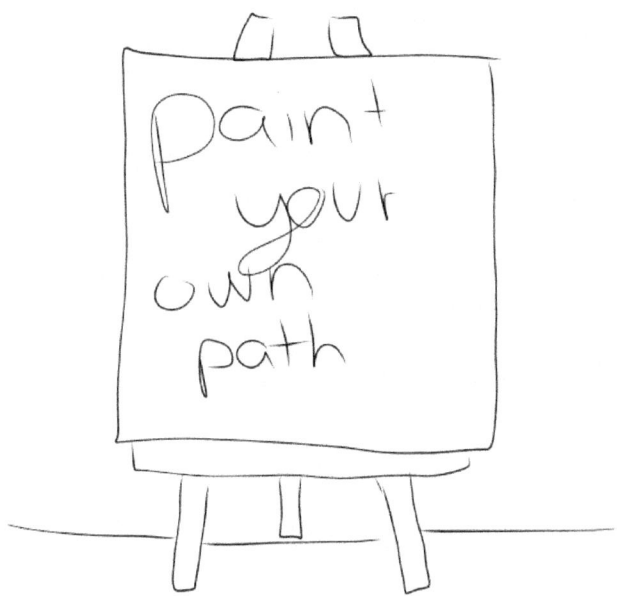

I am a puzzle.

If you find all the pieces

And manage to put me back together

There will always be a piece missing,

Leaving you with a mystery and a story

You'll never get to know.

- Caprice Geddes

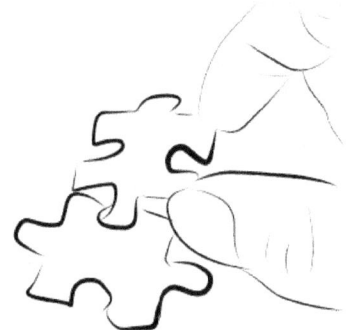

Until I stick a doormat on my clothes

That reads; "open for business",

What I wear does not give you permission

To demand that I give you everything

As you trespass into my home.

- Caprice Geddes

Little Grey Box

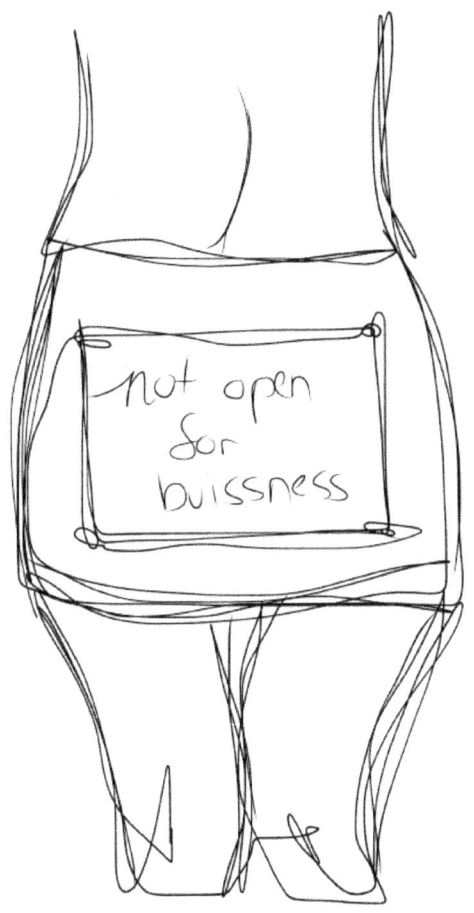

I am sorry I didn't give the truth,

For when I tried to explain

The words ran away.

-    Caprice Geddes

As my head hits the pillow at night

It all comes flowing back

Like a water stream after the heavy rain has fallen

And the flood gates are opened.

It's slow until it rushes

All at once.

- Caprice Geddes

Objects of smaller children have been used to portray

The trapping of an evil spirit

In which comes to life at night

As its mission is to cause

Such terror in the dark.

But for the toys and the teddy bears

That sit quietly above my desk

They are my protectors of such beautiful memories.

For they remind me of a quiet time

As a child where throwing dinner parties

For my toys and family

Brought us such joy.

But now the dinners are filled

with silence so quiet you could hear

The soft humming of the crickets behind the walls

As our eyes never leave what's put in front of us.

- Caprice Geddes

Overcoming your challenges is like climbing a mountain.

For every point you reach you grasp a little more hope

As you are now closer to the top.

When you reach the highest peak

You'll look over to the surrounds

And see the people who have knocked you down

Are still dodging boulders.

- Caprice Geddes

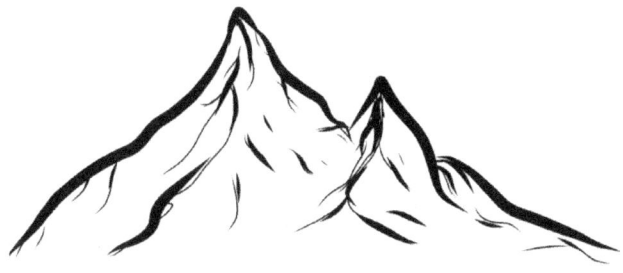

My wall was built so long ago

For every life changing event I added a brick.

Becoming boxed in

As I ran out of land to place the blocked cement.

But if I begin to pick at it

All of what stood will crash down until I am left

With a pile of rubble and nothing

To keep me on my feet.

-    Caprice Geddes

Little Grey Box

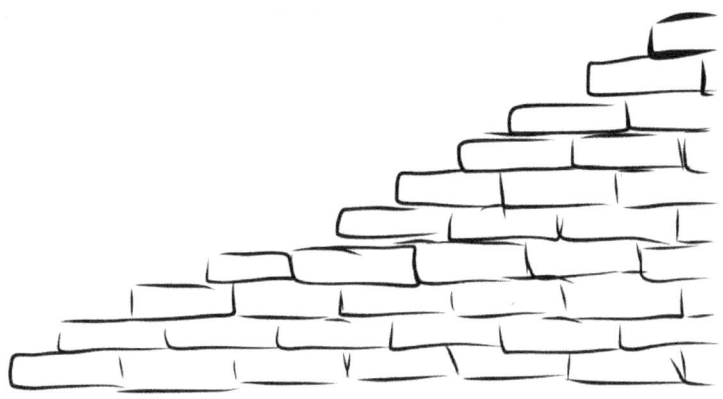

Breath.

What if they don't like me?

Breath.

What if I am a disappointment?

Breath.

What if they expected more?

Breath.

-    Caprice Geddes

Never be afraid of telling people no.

We hid behind the answers that

Will appease people before putting

What we believe is right first

For fear of losing who we care about.

We become so scared to use such a simple

Word yet it could solve many worries.

For if they leave as the word erupts from your mouth

They were not meant to occupy a space in your world.

-    Caprice Geddes

I am the daughter you never bothered to get to know.

The caramel-haired girl that took your eyes as her own

And kept the sorrow of lose burrowed so far no one would know.

She shall not speak of your name for 13 years nor look at the

Only five photos kept as proof of your existence.

For who would want to know such a coward of a man

Set on releasing himself from the pain of a child

By feeding drugs to his own blood as it boiled

Red hot with anger beneath the skin.

The soft eyed girl who was such a burden to your life that a little
Green boat was to set you free of your misery

As your child hung by her feet from the handle

Screaming for her mum as you laughed like the devil.

You were the first man to do wrong by his daughter who had such

Love and hope in her heart for a fairy tale father.

-      Caprice Geddes

A relationship is like the plant your mum bought you

As a child to show her you could keep it from dying

Before purchasing your first pet.

You must tend to it as often as you can

For it to continue blossoming and growing beautifully.

- Caprice Geddes

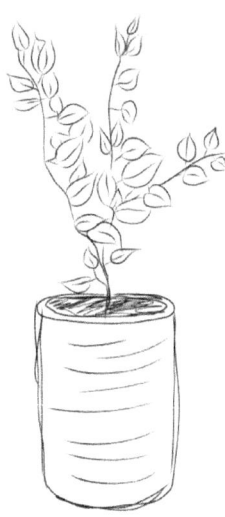

Forgiveness comes to those who work for it.

Even after all you do,

You still don't hear the words 'I forgive you',

At least you know for yourself that you tried.

- Caprice Geddes

I became blind to the love you provided me

For the constant fear of being betrayed before

By those who kept me from my little grey box.

- Caprice Geddes

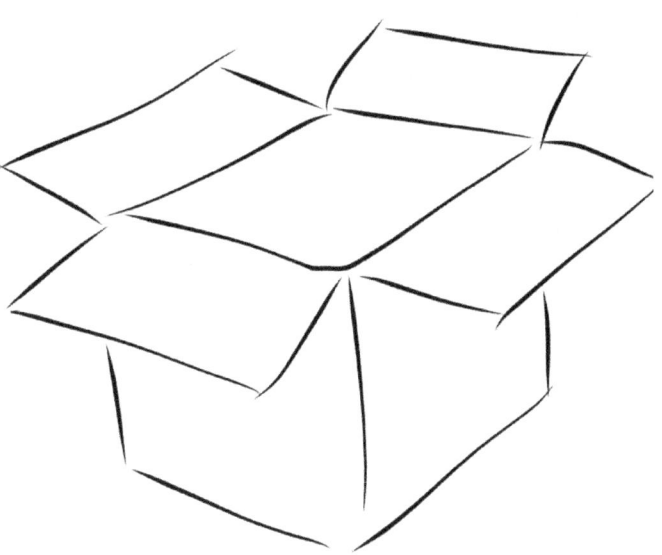

Love is a two-way street

Such as bees and flowers.

To the bee, the flower gives them

A storage of life.

To the flower, the bee is the

Visiting love giving the blessing of

Reproduction.

They are both as important to each other,

As all relationships should be.

-    Caprice Geddes

Once the story had left my mouth,

Everyone else was left in doubt.

- Caprice Geddes

I thought pretty new clothing hid my insecurities

As people were so focused on what look I had today.

Yet I never realized it was my undoing

For the questions that arose

Left me frozen in a trail of my thoughts.

I had edited away what I thought were mistakes

But they were my own flesh and blood,

Making me,

Me.

-    Caprice Geddes

I am so very lucky to be here with you

In the midst of all great discoveries

And mystery yet to be uncovered.

For we are one of them.

- Caprice Geddes

If I pull the piece of thread that hangs with such little life

From the cuff of my sleeve,

It will start to unravel until I am left with

Nothing but a pile of lifeless string.

For it is the same with people.

Pull to hard at someone who Is already fighting

To stay in place,

You'll be left with more than what you started with,

But less of what you want.

-     Caprice Geddes

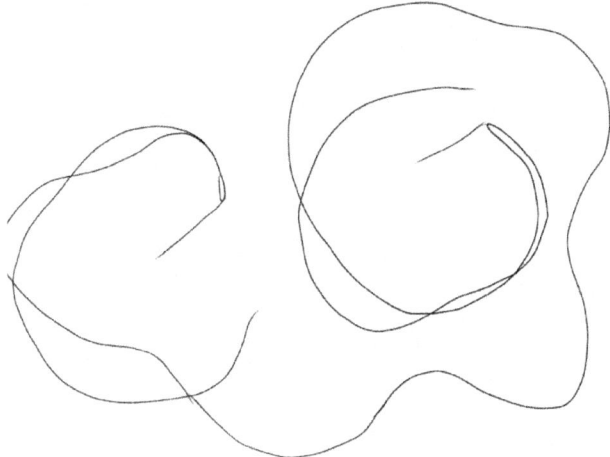

Should I say thank you

For being the first man to teach me

Not to have trust as people come and go.

For you never made the effort to stay,

To show me that not everyone leaves when

Obstacles arise or the unexpected happens.

In reality I should be thanking you for being

The person I never got to know.

As my life took a turn for the better when

I let out my last cry to my mother at the age of three,

For that was the final time I will see you

As we have parted ways until the day I die.

- Caprice Geddes

The loss that has occurred

Shall be a reference point

In your life,

Remembering what such a past

Causes in someone's future.

-       Caprice Geddes

As I climb my tree

I hope to look over and see

You at the top of yours

And as I reach you,

We can continue climbing

Together.

-    Caprice Geddes

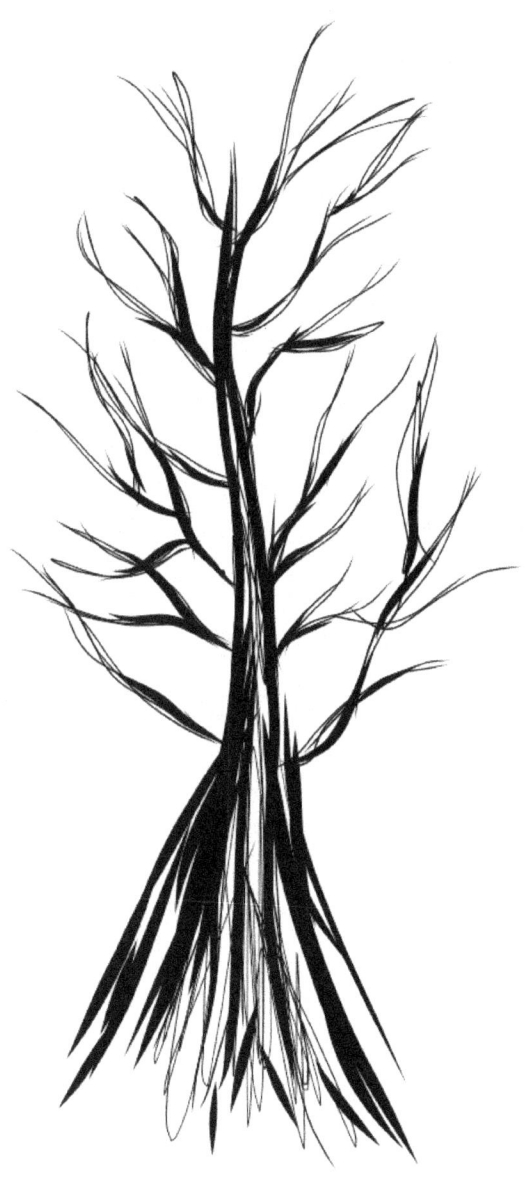

I'm sorry for expecting more,

For I should've remembered you were

Made of 70 percent of empty promises

Sinking to the bottom,

Slowly being forgotten about as it's covered

with more sunken ships of lies.

- Caprice Geddes

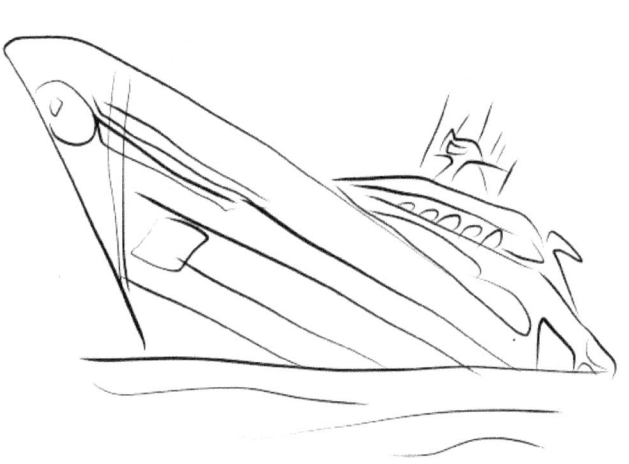

Such a concept of feeling becomes so foreign

After the loss of hope in a father.

For who could abandon an automatic bond

Of unconditional love surfacing

After the first look into the tiniest eyes

said to be yours.

- Caprice Geddes

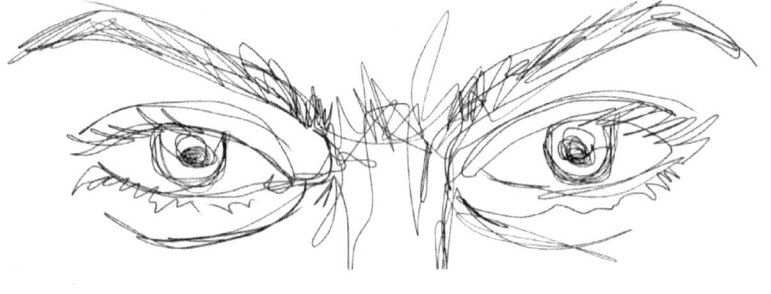

The little voice inside my head

Was my only friend for many years.

It shielded me from what was said

And prevented many tears.

-      Caprice Geddes

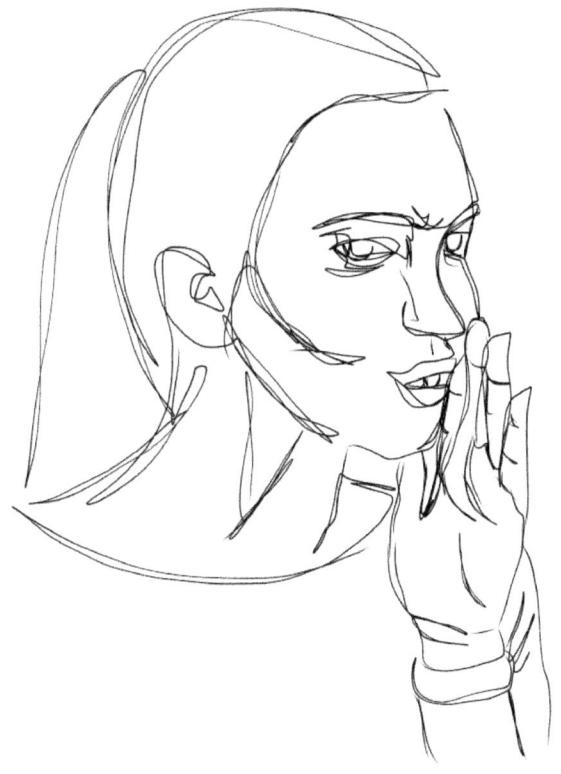

You are the only one who knows

What's going to make you happy,

Whether that's flowers in your hair

Or a piece of paper holding your degree.

Your life is a blank canvas

Still left to be created into YOUR masterpiece.

Don't let anyone else paint it for you.

-     Caprice Geddes

The door was slammed and locked

Leaving me hopeless on the other side

As the torment continued through the heavy

Thin wood.

But as I turned around,

I spotted another of seeming quietness

Like peace to my ears,

For I only dare open slowly

Leaving my troubles behind locked doors.

-     Caprice Geddes

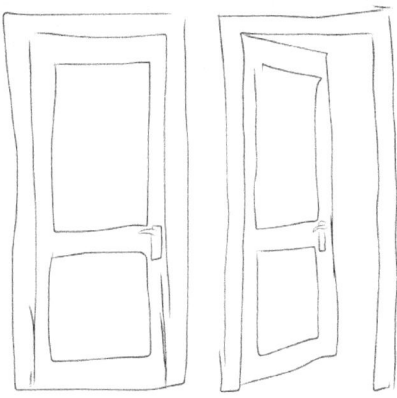

You knew I was fragile,

Yet you let me fall

Watching blank faced

As I hit the ground

Shattering into a pile of useless

Pieces unable to be put back together.

-    Caprice Geddes

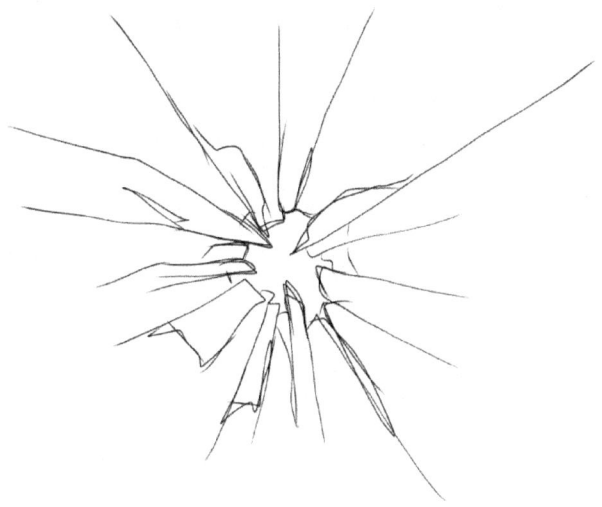

We are told what we weigh should

Now be such a little obstacle.

Yet why after so many years of tried positivity

Those small numbers that light up on a screen

Is enough to alter someone's happiness,

Acting as a switch inside

For a battle to begin.

-    Caprice Geddes

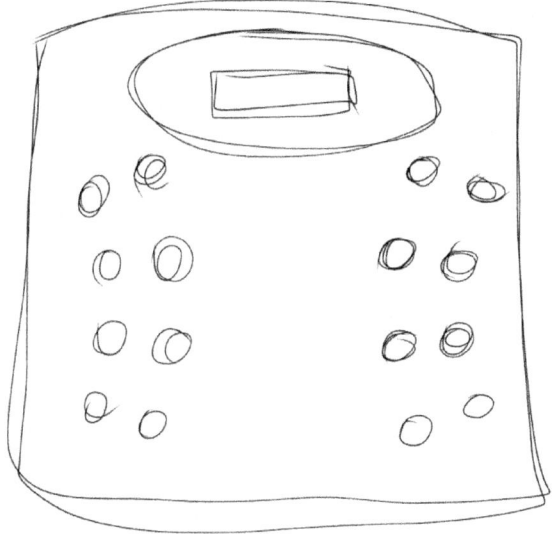

You are a flower my dear,

For flowers hold such purity in their beauty

Making each one unique.

You are that one in a million.

-     Caprice Geddes

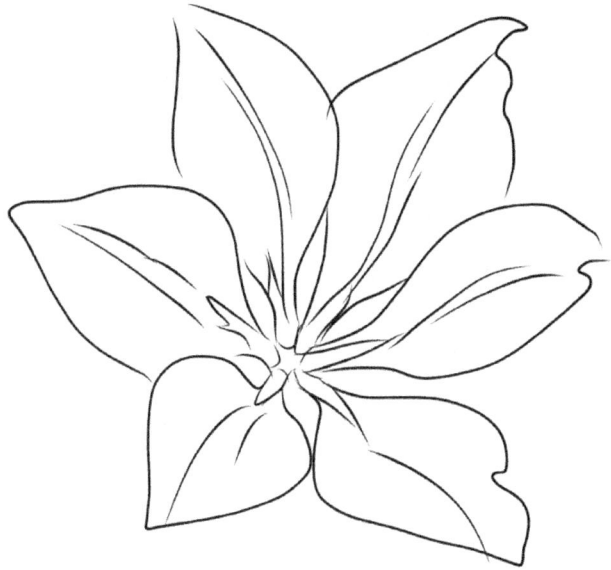

Time was our worst enemy,

hearing the ticking clock in every

Moment of tense silence

Reminding us that it was only a matter

of seconds until hell was released.

- Caprice Geddes

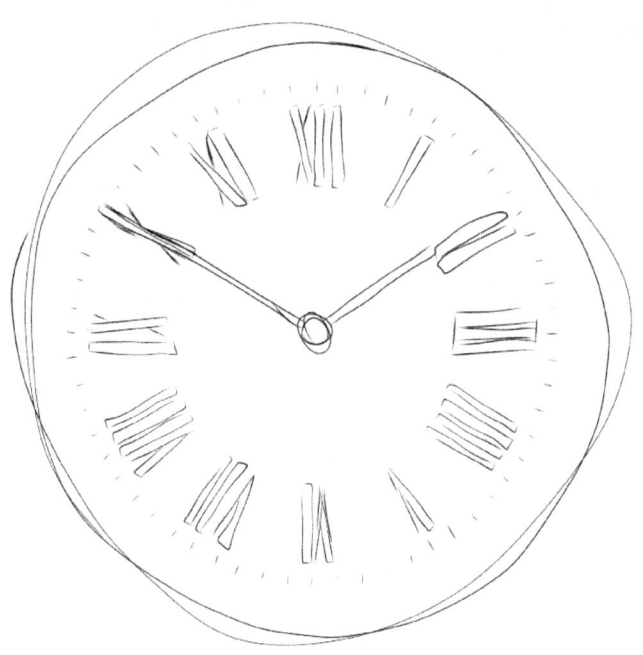

Stay with me.

For I'll be alongside you

In every life time.

-    Caprice Geddes

You held a smile I so often saw,

A smile that could light up an entire room

Or make anyone feel a sense of belief in the good

As the corners of your mouth tilted up.

Now it doesn't leave your face and I question if

The happiness radiated by such a simple action

Now promotes your sadness?

For that smile no longer shows the crinkle

At the sides of your eyes

That had once been admired.

-    Caprice Geddes

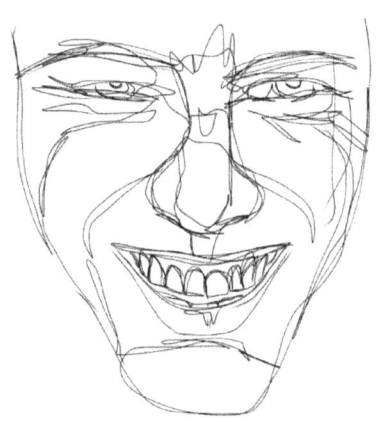

School is not meant to be such a heart racing place

Where getting asked a question

Is like having a gun pressed against your head

Fearing that the trigger will be pulled

If not answered correctly.

-     Caprice Geddes

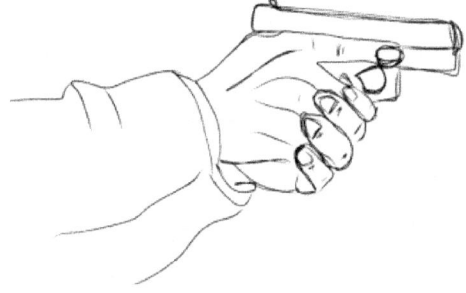

We all have what we believe are flaws,

For we hide them beneath makeup, clothing

And behind the handheld screens,

Thinking about what a wonderful place it would be

If we were taught the subject of self-love and expression

To flaunt what makes us afraid and unique to our world.

-    Caprice Geddes

No one sees the clockwork in your head,

But you feel it.

Every question that requires intense recollection of those moments

The wood clashes together and you can't help but hold you head

With agony.

For your brain has already thought about so much

that a simple question about your day

Would be like writing another school essay.

-    Caprice Geddes

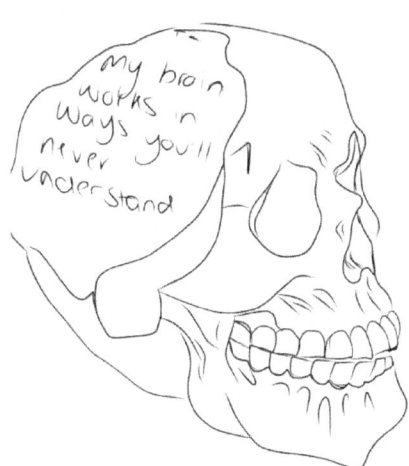

Yes, I'm a little bit of crazy

But I'll be in your box of favourites

Waiting for you to choose me

Within the mix of others at the top

Of the jam-packed cardboard.

Yet you might find me alone at the bottom,

For you always leave the best till last.

- Caprice Geddes

She's going to repeat this cycle

Over and

Over and

Over again.

But she'd do it a million times

For the good she sees left in you

-    Caprice Geddes

Scrabble.

As I place a letter down they

Scrabble.

For each letter I strategically placed they

Scrabble until there is nothing left

But morse code as my eyes strain

To put T and O together.

    Turn1ng

        1nt0

          Num6ers

            And words not yet discovered.

-     Caprice Geddes

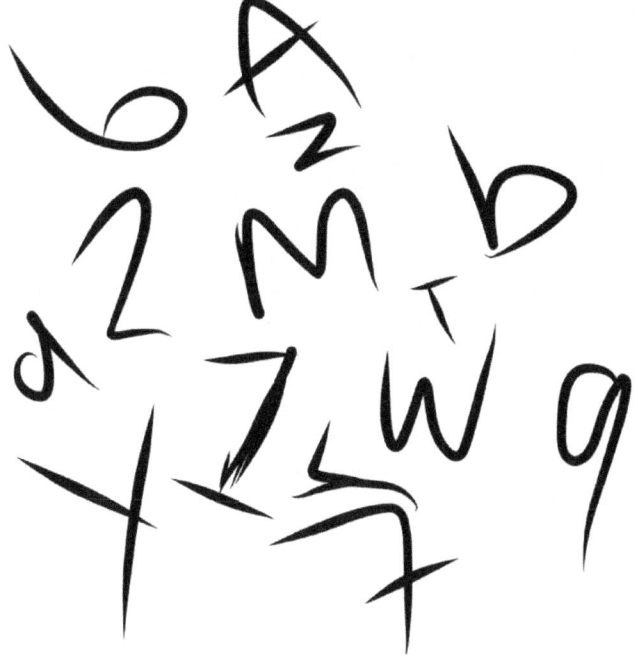

You can still feel the sting of pain

Without the familiar hand against your skin,

For words can do more harm

Than that hand ever did.

As it is mental to feel a fist reaching in

to grab what you kept locked behind bars,

It can still have the psychical effect

We refuse to understand.

-    Caprice Geddes

Let me ask you a question.

What's happened in your past?

Can you change it?

No.

For the health of yourself, let it go.

- Wise words of someone in my life.

Those words affected my outlook in a great sense.

Do not miss out on someone

Who has the power to better your happiness

For the fear of not knowing the future.

If you never learn to give chances to those

Who have not yet disappointed you,

Then what have you got left to enjoy?

-    Caprice Geddes

The game has changed

And for the first time

You weren't the one to roll the dice.

-     Caprice Geddes

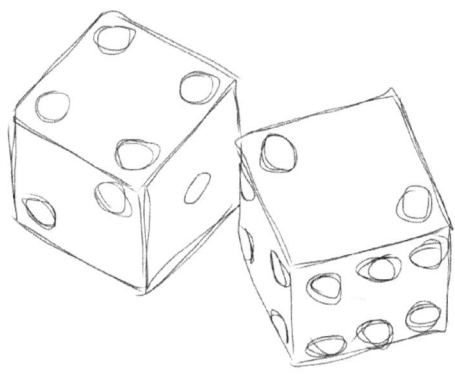

I thank you for keeping your head up high

When I began to lower mine.

Holding my chin up enough for me to catch

Myself lost in your eyes.

Assuring me by such a simple gaze

 everything was going to be okay.

-    Caprice Geddes

If you've ever looked at a car on the road that has caught your eye,

It is only the exterior you are viewing.

For the exterior of a car represents a person so correctly.

The owner spends time and money on paint and details

To appear to the audience admiring from afar

But the inside can remain the same as they will not see it.

A new haircut, outfit and makeup can change

People's perception on your level of attractiveness

While tricking them into believing

They are someone who has changed.

Yet their personality and actions that have caused

Many troubles for others

Remain the same on the interior

And are forgotten while covered.

-    *Caprice Geddes*

On your darkest of days

The sun will still shine down on you

Placing a tiny spot thought of as

A sun kissed mark by the spiritual

To remind yourself each time you look

In the mirror,

Those tiny, aging dots living

On each inch of your skin

Represent another day you got up and fought.

-    *Caprice Geddes*

I am surrounded with such beautiful

People each day

Who inspire me to do my best.

- Caprice Geddes

You'll be living in a high-class home

Sponsored by your parents

For they have money to throw away.

You'll allure a younger woman with

A life still not lived who pities

Your fantasy stories

Of such a horrible wife

With a brat of a kid that was not your own.

She'll bare the miracle of a child

You always wanted,

Showered in gifts and affection from a family

Who wanted nothing but their blood.

And after all we went through,

The two of us will be living with

Such troubles of money and life.

For the world works in cruel ways.

-     Caprice Geddes

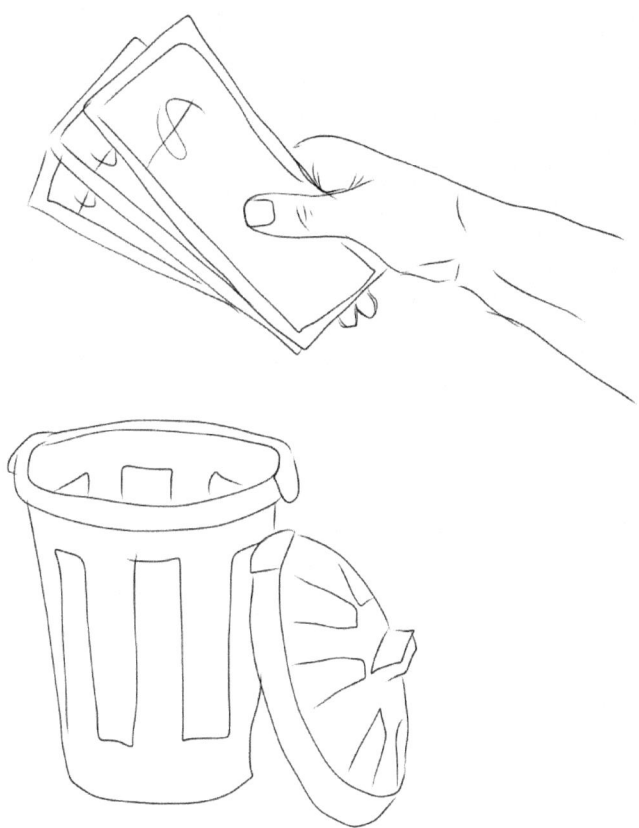

Enjoy every moment

Alongside with the bad ones

For they will remind you how

You faced your worst experience

With strength you never knew.

Each dramatic problem

That crosses your path

Will show you that everything else

Is tiny in comparison,

Not worth worrying about.

Change your outlook

- *Caprice Geddes*

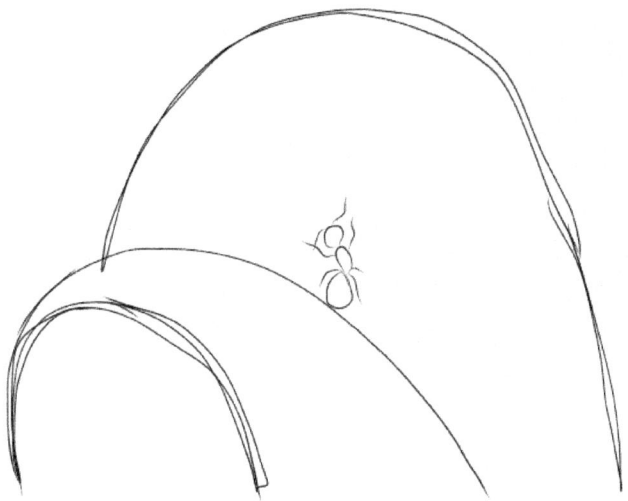

I will not be the first in the line of women

In my family who has gone through hell and back.

I will not be the first who has learnt their level

Of strength and courage through experience of trauma.

I will not be the first in my family who has not let silence

Become their only source of life.

I have had many women before me who have built me up

Since day one to handle the challenges thrown our way

And understand what's worth fighting for.

But I will be the first to use my real name among the pages.

To not hide behind the fear and backlash, but to be a voice

For those whose cry of help are silenced.

And for that,

I am proud of myself.

-      Caprice Geddes

You sat so quietly

But with such purpose.

-    Caprice Geddes

The flower known to represent love is always the first

To die in a bouquet of varieties.

It is given to show affection

From the beauty and colour of red

That eventually turns to a dull black.

Ever wonder if the flower was not just picked

For its beauty and selection of shades,

But picked for the symbol of its lifespan

To remind us that as they sit on our bedside table

The love will eventually die out as the rose

Slowly starts to lose its petals and life.

I was the lucky one

For he and I talked of chrysanthemums.

-    Caprice Geddes

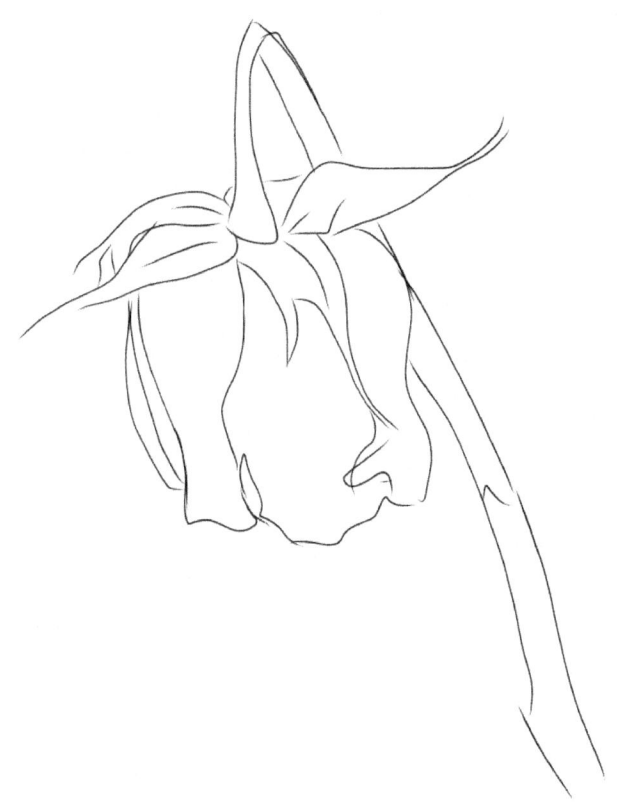

I respect people who stand up for what they believe is right,

Who to trust and cut people off who have wronged them

In unforgiveable ways.

Who don't run back to their old habits because

They're scared of change,

but finding their source of happiness in something new.

I respect the people who risk the back lash to speak

Only the truth to protect one another

And who keep their head up high during the process.

- Caprice Geddes

You were the devil dressed in his clothing

Playing the charade of his nicer past life

To appear normal to anyone one who

Approaches him on outside.

But when you came home

The mask came off and the fire

Burning from the inside had consumed

Who we used to love.

- Caprice Geddes

She told me that all she heard was;

'Now isn't a good time'.

Yet there will never be a good time

For the timer on the bomb

She was about to set on your home

As the words crept from her mouth.

- Caprice Geddes

www.ingramcontent.com/pod-product-compliance
Lightning Source LLC
Chambersburg PA
CBHW072143170526
45158CB00004BA/1489